Amazing Bible Mazes

and Other Puzzles

Written by
Anita Reith Stohs

Illustrated by Andy Willman

CPH
SAINT LOUIS

For Christopher Stohs
Proverbs 3:5–6

Cover illustration by Dennis Jones

Scripture quotations taken from the HOLY BIBLE, NEW INTERNATIONAL VERSION®. NIV®. Copyright © 1973, 1978, 1984 by International Bible Society. Used by permission of Zondervan Publishing House. All rights reserved.

Copyright © 1997 Concordia Publishing House
3558 S. Jefferson Avenue, St. Louis, MO 63118-3968
Manufactured in the United States of America

2   3   4   5   6   7   8   9   10   06   05   04   03   02   01   00   99   98

Adam and the Animals

God created the earth and everything on it, including all the animals. God created humans in His image and asked us to take care of His creation. God brought the animals to the first man, Adam, so he could name them.

These animals need help to find Adam. Begin at the letter C and find the names of the animals pictured here in order. The last letter of the animal's name is the first letter in the name of the next animal. You can move forward and backward, up and down.

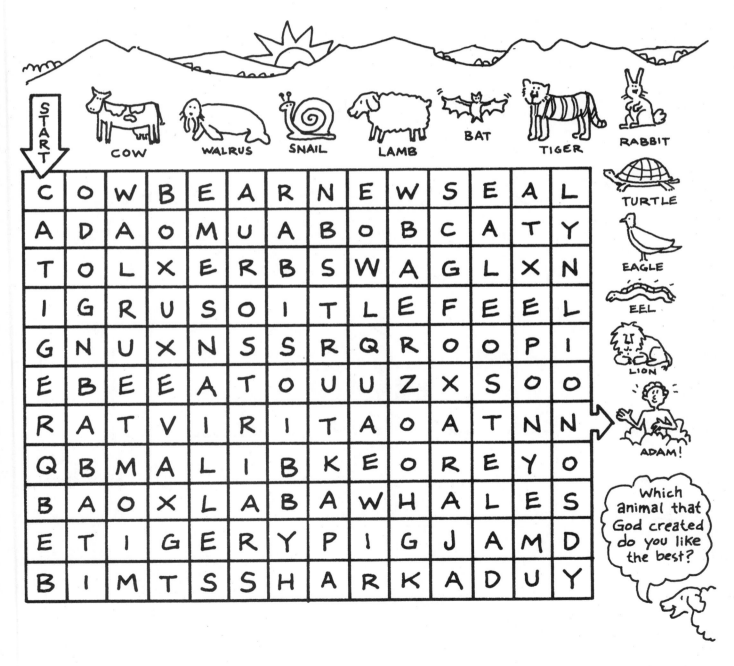

A Rainbow of Hope

God told Noah to build an ark because He was going to send a flood. During the flood, God took special care of Noah, his family, and the animals inside the ark. God takes care of you too. He washed away your sin through the water of Baptism and made you His special child.

After the flood, God put a rainbow in the sky. What do rainbows remind us of? As you find your way through the maze, put the letters your path runs through in the blanks in the ark.

Abraham and Sarah Move to a New Land

God told Abraham and Sarah to move to a new land. He promised to make Abraham's sons and daughters into a great nation. God said that one day the whole world would be blessed through a child born from Abraham's family.

God kept His promises when He sent Jesus to be our Savior. Jesus was a great-great-great … grandson of Abraham and Sarah. Help Abraham and Sarah find their new home.

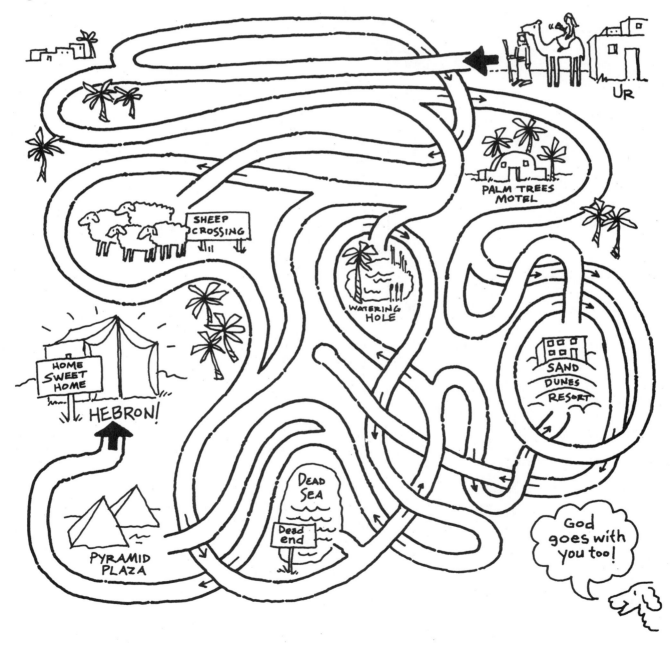

Joseph's Amazing Coat

Jacob gave his son Joseph a beautiful robe. Joseph's brothers were jealous. They sold Joseph into slavery and told Jacob he was dead.

One year there wasn't enough food for Jacob, his sons, and their families. Joseph's brothers went to Egypt to buy food. Joseph was in charge of selling the food. He forgave his brothers and welcomed them, their families, and his father to Egypt.

Find your way through the maze on Joseph's coat. Then use bright crayons to color it.

START

END!

Thank God for a special gift you received.

A Baby in a Basket

Pharaoh ordered his soldiers to kill the baby boys born to the Israelites. Moses' mother hid her son to protect him. She put him in a basket-boat on the Nile River.

Moses' sister, Miriam, watched her little brother. God watched him too. When Pharaoh's daughter found Moses, Miriam offered to get a woman to take care of him. She got her mother. God saved Moses' life.

Moses and the Ten Commandments

God told Moses and the Israelites to camp by Mount Sinai. He told Moses to climb the mountain. God gave Moses His Law. He wrote it on two stone tablets. We call God's Law the Ten Commandments. These commandments tell us how to act toward God and others.

We can't obey the Ten Commandments on our own. But we believe Jesus died for the times we don't follow God's Law. God forgives our sins for Jesus' sake.

Help Moses take the Ten Commandments down the mountain.

Sing a Song of Praise

King David played his harp and sang songs of praise to God. Some of his songs are in the book of Psalms. His most famous song begins "The Lord is my Shepherd."

Find the way through the harp.

A New Temple

God chose King Solomon to build His temple. The people of God worshiped Him in this beautiful building. It was made from the best materials, including gold and cedar wood. The dedication service for the new temple lasted 14 days!

Help the children find their way to the dedication service.

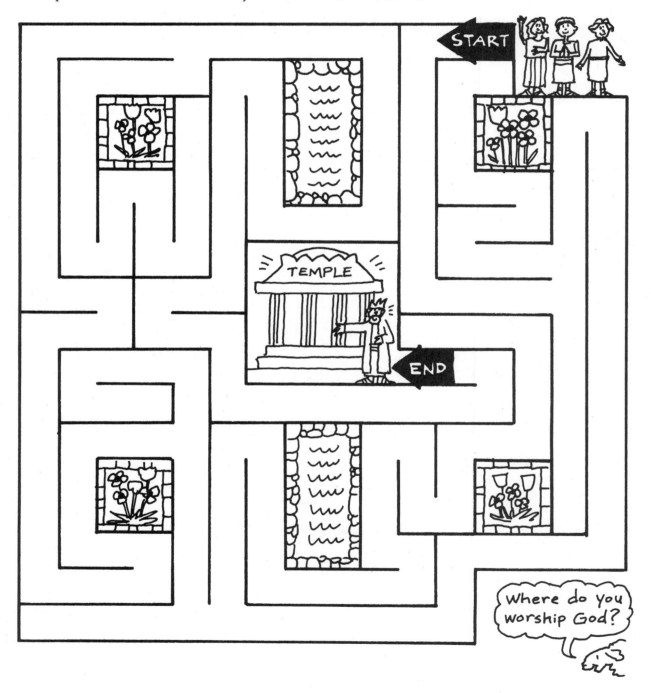

The Lord Feeds Elijah

God told His prophet Elijah to tell the wicked King Ahab that it wouldn't rain. Then God told Elijah to hide by a brook. God sent ravens with meat and bread to feed Elijah. Elijah drank water from the brook.

Help the raven find Elijah. Begin at the top and connect the squares that have pictures of food—for example, pie to pear. The squares should touch on the sides.

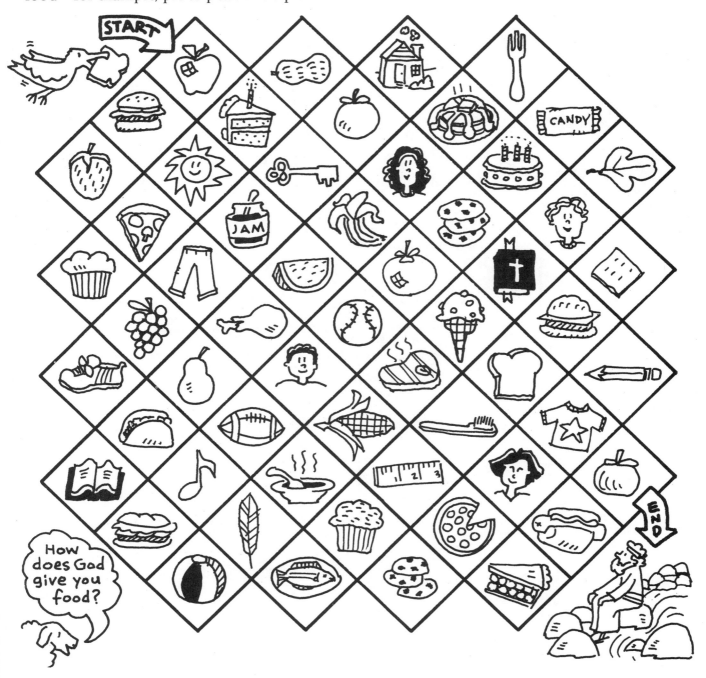

Swallowed by a Fish

God told Jonah to go to Nineveh and tell the people to repent. Jonah took a boat in the opposite direction. But God sent a storm. The sailors were so scared they threw Jonah overboard.

God sent a giant fish to swallow Jonah. Jonah stayed inside the fish for three days, just like Jesus was in the tomb for three days. Jonah prayed for help from inside the fish. God heard his prayer.

Help Jonah find the way out of the fish.

Ask God to help you when it's hard to tell someone about Jesus.

A Queen Who Helped Her People

God's people had been sent to live in Persia. God made a beautiful Jewish woman queen. When a wicked man named Haman wanted to kill God's people, God used this queen to save His people.

Do you know the queen's name? To find her name, follow the lines to put each letter into an empty circle.

God helps you stand up for those being treated unfairly.

Daniel in the Lions' Den

Daniel believed in God. He prayed to God often. The king of Babylon, the land where Daniel lived, commanded everyone to worship him. Daniel obeyed God, not the king.

One day as he was praying, Daniel was arrested. The king threw Daniel in the lions' den. Daniel asked God to help him. God sent His angel to protect Daniel. The lions never opened their mouths.

Take Daniel safely through the lions' den.

The Road to Bethlehem

Before Jesus was born, Mary and Joseph had to travel from Nazareth to Bethlehem. When they got to Bethlehem, they couldn't find a place to stay. Finally, an innkeeper told them they could stay in a stable. While they were there, Jesus was born.

Help Mary and Joseph get to Bethlehem. Starting at the star, connect the squares with Christmas pictures—for example, caroler to wreath.

Joy to the World

The night Jesus was born, God sent an angel to tell some shepherds the good news. The angel said, "Christ the Savior is born." The shepherds were amazed. Then angels filled the whole sky, singing praises to God.

The shepherds hurried to find Jesus. After they worshiped Him, they told everyone they met about the baby born to be our Savior. Help the shepherds find Jesus in the manger.

Follow the Star

God put a star in the sky to announce Jesus' birth. Some Wise Men from the East saw the star and followed it to find Jesus. They brought expensive gifts to worship their King. Can you name the gifts?

Help the Wise Men follow the path that has only stars. It leads to Jesus.

What gift would you have brought to the child Jesus?

Fishers of People

"Come, follow Me," Jesus said to some fishermen. And they did. "Come, follow Me," Jesus says to you. Then He helps you follow His footsteps all the way to heaven.

Help the fishermen get to shore so they can follow Jesus. Connect the shapes that have animals that live in the sea—for example, whale to jellfish.

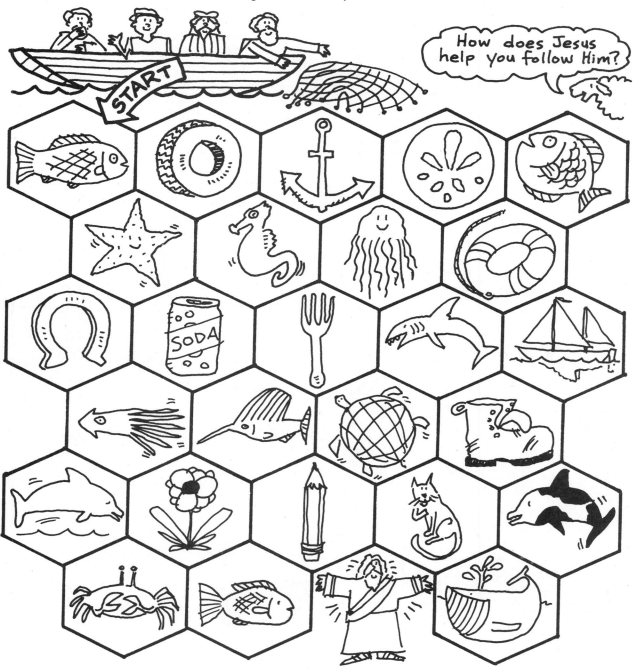

Jesus Blesses the Children

"Go away!" the disciples said to some children and their mothers who had come to see Jesus. "No," Jesus said. "Let the children come to Me." Then Jesus picked the children up and blessed them.

Help the children and their mothers get to Jesus.

Jesus Feeds a Crowd

A large crowd listened to Jesus talk all day. No one remembered to bring food. The disciples found one boy with five loaves of bread and two fish. Jesus thanked God for the food and passed it out to the crowd. There was enough to feed more than 5,000 people!

Find five loaves of bread and two fish that look alike.

Thank God for your favorite food.

Jesus Walks on Water

Jesus' disciples took a boat across the Sea of Galilee. Jesus stayed behind to pray. While the disciples sailed, a storm blew in. The waves smacked into the boat. The disciples were scared.

The disciples saw someone walking on the water. They thought it was a ghost. Then they heard Jesus tell them not to be afraid. When Jesus got in the boat, the wind and waves stopped. "You are the Son of God," the disciples told Jesus.

Help Jesus find the path through the wild waves.

Zacchaeus Meets Jesus

Zacchaeus was too short to see Jesus through the crowd. So Zacchaeus climbed a tree to see Jesus. Jesus knew where Zacchaeus was. He called, "Come down, Zacchaeus! I'm going to your house today."

Help Zacchaeus get down from the tree.

Lost and Found

Jesus told a story about a shepherd who left 99 sheep to look for one that was lost. When he found it, the shepherd carried the sheep home. He was so happy, he called all his friends to celebrate. Jesus said this is how the angels respond when one person becomes a member of God's family.

Help the shepherd find his lost sheep.

A Happy Homecoming

Jesus told a story about a young man who took his share of his father's money and left home. He wasted all his money on fancy things and fun times. He needed a job. The only job the young man could find was feeding pigs.

The young man decided to go home. He planned to ask his father to forgive him and to make him one of his servants. The father forgave his son, but he didn't make him a servant. He threw a party to welcome his son home.

Help the son get back to his father.

24

A Good Helper

Jesus told a story about a man who was robbed and beaten. Two men passed by but did not help the injured man. Finally, a Samaritan stopped. He cleaned the man's wounds and took him to an inn where he could get better.

First, follow the lines to find which man is the Good Samaritan. Then, follow the lines from the injured man to find the right path to the inn.

Ask God to help you help someone today.

Shouts of Praise

"Hosanna to the Son of David," the children shouted as Jesus walked through the temple. Some adults tried to make the children be quiet. But Jesus said the children were supposed to praise Him.

Help the children find Jesus.

Jesus Died for You

Why did Jesus die on the cross? To find the answer, follow the lines to put each letter in a blank square.

Jesus Is Alive!

Early on the first Easter morning, Mary Magdalene went to Jesus' tomb. When she got there, the stone had been rolled away and the tomb was empty. She cried because she thought someone had taken Jesus' body.

Then Mary saw someone. She thought He was the gardener, but it was Jesus. She ran back and told the disciples Jesus was alive.

Help Mary get to Jesus' empty tomb.

How would you have felt if you were Mary?

Good News for All People

"Make disciples of all nations," Jesus said to His followers before He returned to heaven. Jesus gives you that same job. You tell others about Jesus by the way you act and talk. Ask Jesus to help you show others His love through your words and actions.

Help each set of children reach Jesus.

Jesus Changes Saul's Life

Saul went to Damascus to find Christians and put them in jail. Jesus met Saul along the road and changed his life! When Saul finally got to Damascus, he asked to be baptized. God had worked faith in Saul's heart.

Saul later changed his name to Paul. God used him to tell many people about Jesus. Paul was one of the first Christian missionaries.

Help Saul get to Damascus. On the way, he'll pass Jesus.

A Safe Shipwreck

The ship was stuck on a sandbar, but it was too far from shore. The waves crashed into the ship. The waves broke the ship into pieces. The soldiers, prisoners, and sailors were afraid of dying. Paul told them, "Not one of you will lose a single hair from your head."

Everyone who could swim jumped overboard and swam to land. Those who couldn't swim grabbed pieces of the ship and floated to shore. God kept everyone safe.

Help Paul and the others reach land.

Jesus Is the Way

"I am the way and the truth and the life," Jesus said. "No one comes to the Father except through Me." Jesus won forgiveness for your sins on the cross. Because Jesus came back to life, you will live in heaven with Him forever.

Draw a picture of yourself next to Jesus. Then find the path to heaven.